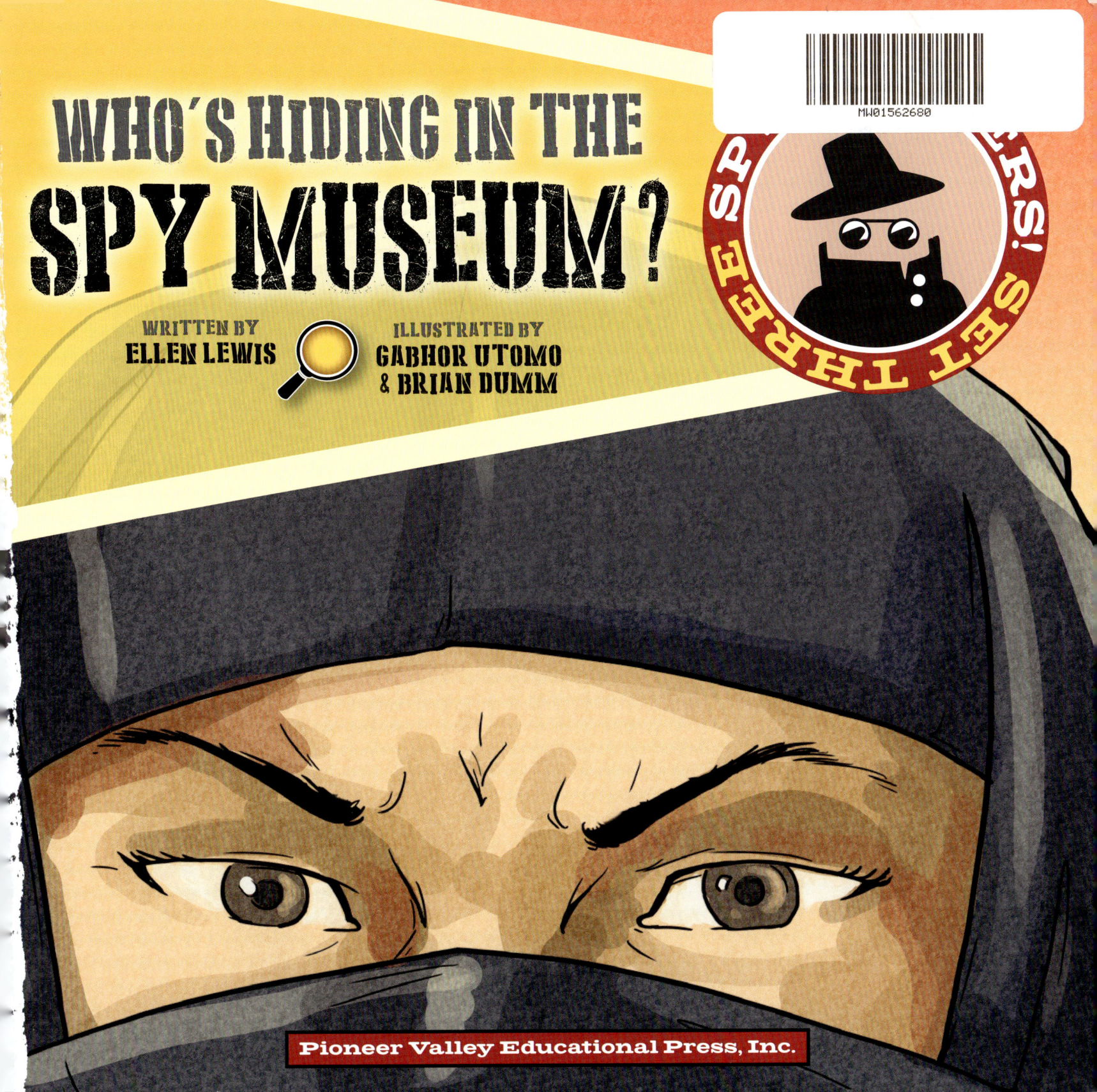

Kayla and Tim smiled. In the past few months, they had gotten to know Ms. Keel—first as a tour guide on their museum field trip, and then as a mentor. She had instructed them about the first skill any spy learns — observation. By using the skill of observation, they had helped solve a number of spy cases.

The International Spy Museum was their favorite place now, and they discovered new things every time they returned. Besides observation, they had learned about dead drops, brush passes, ciphers, codes, and bugs and listening devices.

"Anyway, didn't you say you wanted to do something new this week? How about a trip through our ductwork?"

"Cool!"

"Let's do it!"

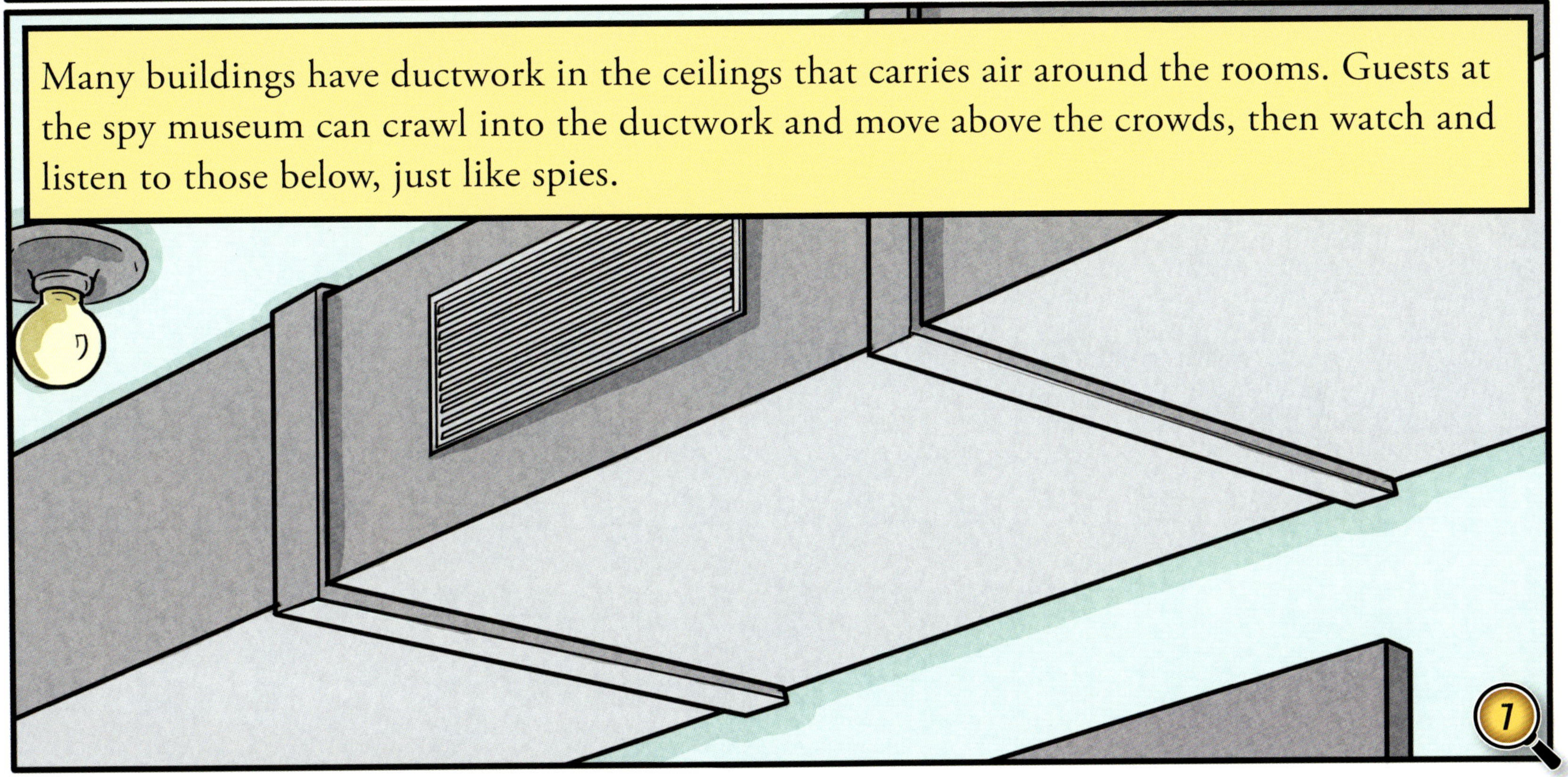

Many buildings have ductwork in the ceilings that carries air around the rooms. Guests at the spy museum can crawl into the ductwork and move above the crowds, then watch and listen to those below, just like spies.

The adventure starts in the Bugs and Listening Devices area. Visitors climb stairs and crawl along the ductwork as it snakes across the ceiling. The ductwork ends at another set of stairs near the Disguise Gallery in the School for Spies area. Visitors often hear the banging and clanging of kids in the metal ducts overhead. Kids can hear people below and can spy on them through grills built into the duct's metal walls.

Kayla and Tim climbed the stairs and followed the signs into the ductwork.

They got down on all fours and snaked through the dark, three-foot-wide passage. Every ten feet, a grill let in some light from below.

"It's very peculiar. Let's clear our minds by doing something else."

"Did you do the reading I gave you about the different kinds of spies?"

"Cloak, dagger, shadow, and... what was the other one?"

"Ninja!"

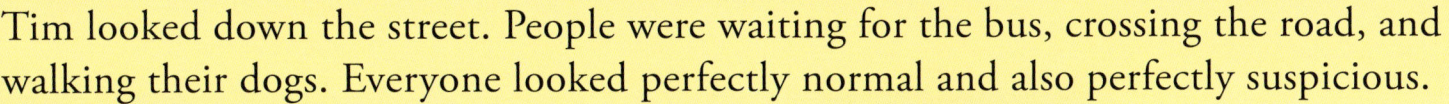

Tim absentmindedly moved his hand toward the ninja's feet. Without thinking, he touched the mannequin's slipper-covered foot.

"Wow, this is so realistic. It feels like a real foot."

"Tim! You can't touch the mannequin!"

Are you OK?

We're fine!

Is the mannequin supposed to do that?

No, Kayla. I think you just found our ghost.

It didn't take long to find the real mannequin hidden under the platform.

Ms. Keel showed them how the wall behind the ninja display could be opened and closed like a hidden door. It helped the museum to move large display items.